Living UNSTUCK

by
Anita Hunt & Jeannie Bruenning

Live the joy!
Anita Hunt
Jeannie Bruenning

FIRST SILVER THREAD PUBLISHING EDITION, JANUARY 2018
Silver Thread Publishing is a division of A Silver Thread, Pismo Beach, CA.
www.asilverthread.com
Text Copyright © 2017 Hunt Bruenning
http://livingunstuck.us
Cover image by WavebreakPremium
All images used by approval
ISBN 978-0-9991794-3-7
Printed in the United States of America

To those who find themselves stuck,
may the words on these pages
give you the courage and determination
to live a life of joy.

Who We Are

Anita Hunt

Anita was born to first generation Americans. Her grandparents were Jewish immigrants from Poland and Russia. She was raised in the Jewish faith. A half century later, Anita was formally introduced to the New Testament and Jesus Christ. It was several years before she fully embraced the whole story; the greatest story ever told.

Before retiring, Anita had the privilege of working in the Real Estate/Mortgage industry. She was honored to assist families in achieving the American dream of owning their own home. In the last few years of her career, she became a trainer and coach. She shared her knowledge with the upcoming generation of mortgage professionals and realized her calling was to help people flourish.

One morning on a walk with her friend, Jeannie, she came to the realization that her passion for writing, love of God's word and desire to coach was the plan that God had for her.

Anita is married, has four children, nine grandchildren and is living her happily ever after in Southern and Central California.

Blog: www.theoccasionaljew.com

Jeannie Bruenning

After working in the corporate business world for over three decades, Jeannie started a boutique publishing company in a small beach town on the central coast of California. The company has always been family run, alongside her husband and two grown children. Being an author herself of six books, she is also passionate about the writer's journey. You can find her most days working and taking conference calls in her Jeep Wrangler, parked on the beautiful sands of Pismo Beach, California.

Jeannie married her childhood best friend; they have two children and a plethora of grandkids. A Pentecostal preacher's kid who is grateful for the love of scriptures her parents instilled, Jeannie loves bringing Biblical truths to our practical lives.
A Silver Thread. Established 2009.

jeanniebruenning.com
asilverthread.com

Why UNSTUCK?

The brothers Gibb wrote a song called Emotions.

You've got me feeling emotion
Deeper than I've ever dreamed of
You've got me feeling emotion
Higher than heaven above

The song was referring to being in love, which we all know is a wonderful emotion. But, what happens when your emotions of love turn to emotions of longing or when feeling fabulous turns to fear or joy to jealousy?

Most of us experience wonderful emotions in life, unfortunately it's human nature to dwell on the not so wonderful ones from time to time. There's nothing wrong with having feelings, but should we get stuck on the negative ones, they have a tendency to overshadow the plans that God has for our life.

The Bible says in the Book of Jeremiah 29:11

"For I know the plans I have for you, says the Lord, they are plans for good and not for disaster, to give you a future and a hope."

The Living Unstuck philosophy is based on Bible verses like Jeremiah 29:11. We believe that God has given a lifetime of promises, that if we truly believe, we can live unstuck lives.

A Personal Story from Anita

When I was young, I attempted to learn how to water ski. I put on my life jacket, pushed my feet into the ski's and learned all the hand signals I would need to communicate with my friends on the boat. In the beginning, I had trouble standing up on the skis, but with some practice, I eventually was able to pop right out of the water. Nothing to it, I thought, this is great!

I was content with my success and enjoyed myself immensely. I thought, now this is the sport of my dreams. Then, I noticed the flailing hand signals from my co-skiers instructing me to move my body outside of the boat's wake.

That didn't seem hard, so I moved my right leg outside of the wake as instructed. But, when I tried to move my left leg over to join my right one, I realized I didn't have enough strength. I couldn't muster up the momentum to get my leg over the frothy water. No matter how many times I attempted to catapult my body over to join my right leg, I failed. My arms were on fire and my legs were shaking. My teeth hurt from clenching them so tightly.

Meanwhile, my friends on the boat were laughing hysterically. They had no idea I was terrified.

Straddling the wake at top speed, I continued to attempt to bring my legs together. They only got further apart. I felt as though I was going to break in half, not to mention how ghastly I looked as a skier. I was trying so hard to reach my goal that I didn't realize my solution was an easy one; just let go of the rope.

There are many emotions that can sometimes cause us to leave the path of our dreams. Like me, you may also get stuck from time to time. Whether it's physical or emotional, it's not always easy to get unstuck. Within these chapters, we will be discussing some of those feelings and offer various tools to help let go of the rope and practice having the life that you want for yourself. So you can live the life that God wants for you, both legs outside of the wake—UNSTUCK!

UNSTUCK TOOLS AND RULES

The Study Sections

In this study there are three chapters. Within each chapter are three studies. Each chapter is focused on different stories from the Bible. They are rich with lessons that apply to us today.

Living Unstuck can be enjoyed as a daily study over several weeks or be explored at your own pace, according to your own personal schedule.

At the conclusion of each study, there is an **Unstuck Challenge**. These challenges are designed to help us change unhealthy thought patterns and propel us forward in our desire to live Unstuck. Give yourself permission to spend the time you need to grow and move forward Unstuck.

Taking Action!

At the end of each study there is a section titled, *Taking Action*. These are activities for you to complete at your own pace to reinforce what you have learned.

We're going to get creative and use mental images in 'Can You Imagine' and 'The Why Game.' We'll bring back memories from our past in a lesson called 'Replay', and we'll talk to the kid in us in 'A letter from a Child.'

In the back of the book, under the title of Unstuck Tools and Rules, you will find more detailed instructions on these activities, as well as several blank pages to record your Aha Moments.

Looking at our Past

We refer to and explore our past for two reasons:
1.   To understand why we react and respond in certain ways, and
2.   To bring healing and forgiveness to past experiences.

We should never bring the past forward. We should never use it as an excuse for our "Stuck-ness."

Meeting in a Group

Unstuck is a wonderful study to do in a small group. If you are in a group setting, confidentiality is essential. What is shared in Unstuck, stays in Unstuck.

We recommend the Unstuck Facilitator Guide if meeting in a group setting.

Bigger than You and I

There are some experiences that are bigger than you or me. If at any time you are feeling overwhelmed, fearful, or anxious, we encourage you to seek professional help. Find someone who can walk alongside you and support you in your journey to becoming Unstuck.

LIVING UNSTUCK

STUDY OUTLINE:

1   Chapter 1: Fearful or Courageous
         The Story of David & Goliath

   4   Part 1: Fear
17   Part 2: Doubt
29   Part 3: Courage

41   Chapter 2: Get Out of God's Way
         The Story of Sara & Hagar

45   Part 1: Effort vs. Action
53   Part 2: Easy vs. Lazy
62   Part 3: The Unleavened Life

73   Chapter 3: Me, Myself and I
         The Story of Cain & Abel

75   Part 1: Anger and Wrath
84   Part 2: Forgiveness
90   Part 3: Learning to Trust

102   The Final Act: Joy

109   Unstuck Tools and Rules

114   References

Aha Moments Journal Pages

CHAPTER 1

FEAR OR COURAGE

Story from the Bible: David and Goliath
1 Samuel 17&18

The story of David and Goliath is a story filled with fear, doubt, and faith. David, the youngest of eight of Jesse's sons, spent most of his young life in the fields with his father's flocks of sheep. When war broke out, David's three older brothers joined the ranks.

The battle between the Philistines and Israel came down to this; Goliath, a giant of a man, against the entire army of Israel. Goliath intimidated the Israelites with shield and javelin in hand, and his savage threats caused the king to retreat out of fear.

Meanwhile, Jesse sends David to deliver provisions to his brothers and bring news of how the battle was progressing. David arrived at the battlefield and heard the battle cry and ran towards it. He witnessed firsthand Goliath's threats that had forced his king and brothers to retreat.

David was incensed, "What will be done for the man who kills this Philistine? For who is this Philistine, that he should taunt the Israelite Army?"

David's brothers were less than thrilled by his questions, and King Saul paid no attention to this young, small boy. However, David keeps pushing forward.

David says to King Saul, "Twice I was tending my father's sheep when a lion and a bear came and took a lamb from the flock. I went after them and attacked and rescued the lamb from their mouth and when they rose against me, I struck and killed them. Yes, I did, this little servant has killed both the lion and the bear. The Lord who delivered me from the paw of the lion and from the paw of the bear will also deliver me from the hand of this Philistine, since he has taunted the armies of the living God."

David persuaded the king to allow him to take on the Giant and once again runs toward the challenge. He was equipped with a stick, a pouch containing five smooth stones, a slingshot, and his unwavering faith in his God.

King Saul also tried to equip David. He clothed David with garments and armor, but when David tried to move under the weight, he said to Saul, "I can't even walk with these and have had no time to test them," and he took the armor off.

When Goliath saw David walking toward him, he mocked him for he was but a youth. Goliath ranted to David, "Am I a dog, that you come to me with sticks? Come to me, and I will give your flesh to the birds of the sky and the beasts of the field."

David said to the Philistine, "You come to me with a sword, a spear, and a javelin, but I come to you in the name of the Lord, the God of the armies of Israel, whom you have taunted. This day the Lord will deliver you into my hands, and I will strike you down... that all the earth may know that there is a God in Israel. The Lord does not deliver by sword or by spear for the battle is the Lord's and He will give you into my hands."

When Goliath came to fight, David ran toward the battle line to meet him. David put his hand into his bag, took a stone and slung it, striking Goliath. The stone sank into the giant's forehead, and he fell to the ground.

David prevailed over the Philistine with a sling and a stone and killed him; there was no sword in David's hand.

Three times in this story we read, "he ran toward...". When everyone else, including the king, was retreating in fear, David ran forward with his faith.

David's doubt had long ago been replaced with fearless faith. God had already tested and proven Himself to this young boy when he was out in the fields and killed the lion and bear. David didn't need God to show him that He was there and would protect him. God already had done that - and David remembered.

The story of David and Goliath is one of the more familiar stories in the Bible. This story is filled with depths of discovery; fear of a King, doubts of an army, and the faith of a boy.

PART I
Fear

Definition:

FEAR is a distressing emotion aroused by impending danger, evil or pain. It doesn't even matter whether the threat is real or imagined, it can evoke a feeling of dread and alarm or a condition of being afraid or apprehensive.

However afraid we are of fear, the truth is we need it. It is an essential part of our lives for obvious reasons of basic survival. It is fear that stops us from walking into traffic, or leaning too far over a railing. Our natural fear instinct was designed to keep us safe when danger confronts us.

So you're telling me Fear is our friend?

It's not the friend one would wish to take on vacation, skydiving, or to a birthday party. Nevertheless, it is our friend. We absolutely do need fear in order to protect us from actual dangers of this world. It is here to protect us, NOT to keep us trapped.

Some of us have allowed Fear to overstep its boundaries. It is no longer acting like a guide, but rather a taskmaster. It would love nothing more than to control our life's path. If we allow it, Fear would be at every turn.

We have to make friends with Fear and like a spoiled child, we must teach it that it is not in control. Rather, Fear has a purpose and we expect it to get a grip and line up to that purpose. Fear out of control can take hold of our entire life.

It is an important emotion, but like all emotions, it needs to be controlled. If allowed the freedom to reign, reign it will! In doing so, Fear will ruin the marvelous, abundant, creative, joy-filled life that God intended.

Being fearful isn't always a bad thing. It helps avoid accidents and can keep us out of harm's way. But when being afraid or overcome with worry becomes a way of life, it inevitably will negatively affect our happiness and the happiness of those around us.

What's Your Perspective?

Can you think of a time when you were living in fear?

Are you still living with fear?

Have you ever experienced panic attacks?

If so, how long did they last?

Have you found yourself unwilling to try new things because of fear?

Has fear prevented you from using your talents and skills the way they were meant to be used?

Have you told anyone about your fears?

If so, were they supportive?

A Personal Story from Anita

I can't count how many times I've been paralyzed with fear in my life. Some of the fear came from things my parents taught me, probably for my own good. Some came from things my parents or friends were afraid of themselves. My mother, for instance, was deathly afraid of thunder and lightening, and driving on mountain roads. So, of course, some of those fears I inherited. In addition, I developed and battled with my own imaginary fears.

After my husband and I were injured in an accident, I could no longer ride in a car without fear or anxiety. If he came home even a few minutes late, I worked myself up into a dither imagining something horrific had happened to him. I even started formulating his obituary. It was so morbid, when he came home, I couldn't bring myself to tell him about it.

It's not just riding in a car that has caused me anxiety; I have a huge fear of spiders and bees. Time and time again, they have feasted on my skin. I've had welts on my body the size of Detroit.

I've been terrified to go places I've never been before. I've been petrified to rent a car in a strange city. Getting lost was catastrophic!

I was nervous to introduce myself in public or speak in front of a group. Just saying my name out loud left me light headed.

I never imagined that I'd have the guts to go snow skiing, zip lining or kayaking. Thankfully, when those occasions did arise, I sheepishly joined in even with trepidation and jitters.

I can't actually say that it was great fun at first. I eventually had a good time and great memories!

One courageous day, my husband and I signed up for a kayak tour up the Huleia River in Kauai. I was apprehensive at first so the guide gave us a tandem Kayak. Having Terry sitting in front of me gave me courage. The oddest feeling came over me. I realized that I was having a good time; so good that I forgot to be afraid. After about an hour of paddling upstream our guide led our group to the banks of the river.

"Who wants to swing from a rope over the river?" our guide asked.

The only person that answered was me. "I don't," I exclaimed.

I watched each kayaker tie their boat to a stump and jump ashore. A few moments later, to my surprise, my husband got out of our kayak, handed me his oar and joined the rest of the crazies that were trying to kill themselves. I was the only one left in any of the boats. I watched as each person took turns, one by one climbing up the side of a tree, grabbing the dangling rope and shouting, "Geronimo" as they swung themselves over the river. Each person hung on for dear life as the rope flung high into the air. They let go and catapulted themselves into the icy water, just like Indiana Jones. I got soaked as their bodies smacked the water. I applauded as they rose to the surface gasping for breath. I was quite relieved when the last person was done and no one had died.

The chanting began. "A-nee-ta, A-nee-ta." Terry grabbed my hand and pulled me from the boat. No, I thought, this isn't happening to me. My heart began to race and everything from that moment became a blur.

Well, I have to tell you, I've conquered these fears by living through them. I've been stung by bees, eaten alive by mosquitos, jumped into rivers and yes, flown off trees. I've kayaked in the ocean and went on trips on the back of motorcycles and believe it or not... I wouldn't trade any of it!

As for introducing myself in public, I became a national trainer and traveled throughout America. I've flown, rented cars and traveled alone at night. I've been the speaker, instructor and facilitator of classes with dozens of people in attendance. I've parked in lots when I wasn't even sure I was at the right building, let alone in the right city.

It took decades before I realized I didn't need to carry a burden of fear. I know now that God didn't want a fearful life for me. I made a conscious decision to pray for strength to release me of my constant fears. I put my trust in Him and felt my burden lift. From time to time, fear creeps back, but then I remember, like David, and I fear no more.

It took all the courage I could muster to begin my journey to get UNSTUCK! Believe me, If I can do it, you can, too!

A Personal Story from Jeannie

Over the course of many years, I had allowed fear to conquer bits of my life until one day I woke up and was afraid to leave home. I was overcome with the fear of something bad happening when I walked out the door. Finally, after years of trying to overcome this fear, I had enough. I decided to think back to the very first time I felt this kind of fear.

It took me awhile to remember fearful situations as a young mother, or earlier as a teen. It was only then I recalled my first panic attack.

I had a best friend at church and each Sunday we would take turns going to each other's house after church. It was my Sunday to go to her house. We had left church and were parked in the parking lot of the grocery store while her mom ran in to pick up a few things.

As we sat there, I felt the heat of fear begin to flow through my body. I started to panic. I broke into a sweat. I turned to my dear friend and said, "I can't come with you". I opened the door and ran two blocks home. As I replayed this scene in my mind, I heard myself say as I grabbed onto my dad's leg, "I'm safe."

"That's it!" I shouted. "I decided as a kid that the only safe place was AT HOME!" Tears rolled down my face as the Fear which had controlled me for so long began to lose its grip. "I'm safe anywhere! God isn't just at home, He's on the plane and in the car; He's at work and at church. He's wherever I go!!!"

In an instant, Fear lost its hold on that part of my life. That isn't to say that Fear didn't try to rear its head from time to time, but I now had a response, "I am safe where ever I go, because God is with me."

Because I had allowed this Fear to live in me for so long, I had some learned behaviors I needed to address. Each time I felt Fear try to take control, I told myself that "I am safe wherever I go because God is with me."

Retraining our minds and reactions can take some time, but they can be retrained.

UNSTUCK CHALLENGE

In order to truly free ourselves of fear, we need to understand where it started. That requires looking back to find its point of conception. Living through past experiences can be painful. Our focus cannot be on others, rather on who we are.

The challenge in this lesson is to do some soul searching. Pick a fear, any fear, and look back to when you first remember experiencing it. This is not to point blame or find fault, rather to understand ourselves and in doing so, free us.

When you find that point, you will be able to see the situation with clarity from a new perspective.

This is a tool that we call Re-Play which you'll find on page 112.

Once the root of that fear is discovered, begin filling your mind and heart with God's promises:

You can go to bed without fear:
You will lie down and sleep soundly.
You need not be afraid of sudden disaster
Or of the destruction that comes upon the wicked;
For the Lord will be your security.
He will keep your foot from being caught in a trap.
Proverbs 3:24-26

Taking Action!

Journaling

Finding a Starting Point

How do you eat an elephant? One bite at a time. How do you conquer fear? One fear at a time.

Start small, take little bites of the elephant called fear.

Example: I overcook my chicken 'cause I'm afraid if I don't, it will have terrible bacteria that could make my family sick.'

Safety in food preparation is important, but there is no excuse for dry chicken!

> Has anyone actually become ill from my chicken?
> Is this a fear passed down from my mother?
> Do I really need to be fearful of undercooked chicken?

This may seem like a silly example - unless you do overcook your chicken - but you can begin to see where our fears come from. Most of the time, they are things we've learned to fear.

As you journal this week, trace the heritage of your fears.
> Where and when did they start?
> Why are you fearful?

Can you Imagine?

Fearless Adventurers!

(Please refer to page 109 in the Unstuck Tools and Rules.)

Today, we're going to imagine ourselves as Fearless Adventurers. We are going to combat our fears by putting on a Cape of Courage.

When you feel that fear is doing everything possible to stop you, then STOP! - literally!

> Ask yourself what the Fearless Adventurer in you would do?
> How should you react?
> What should you say to FEAR?
> Are you going to allow fear to keep you STUCK?

Try it! you have nothing to lose, but FEAR.

Keep track of the FEARS you've conquered.

Confessions

Is there someone in your life you see as a Fearless Adventurer?
What are their characteristics?

Circle the words on the opposite page that exemplify this Fearless Adventurer.

confident

hesitant

gutsy

apprehensive

serious

shy

frightened

tough

bold

nervous

curious

self-conscious

wise

timid

uninteresting

discouraged

awesome

organized

needy

hot-headed

sheepish

nervy

afraid

agitated

playful

spiritless

suspicious

strong

happy

tense

common

frightened

pleasant

sincere

sassy

panicky

chicken

sure

unreliable

disturbed

silly

exciting

anxious

monotonous

spirited

nervous

smart

positive

fun-loving

dreary

dull

upset

courageous

sad

close-minded

daring

negative

frantic

inspiring

joyful open-

minded

controlling

unorganized

interesting

scared

unafraid

thankful

angry

unexciting

mad

tedious

friendly

enjoyable

complainer

Godly

fearless

honest

lost

judgemental

assured

reliable

drab

adventurous

vengeful

Did You Know?

There are many references in the Bible to "Fear Not!" Most of them precede a visit from a celestial being. God knows our human reaction to the unknown will most likely be fear, and He assures us over and over again, do not be afraid.

"What we call the fear of God in scripture is not terror or
dread but an awe that holds God in reverence."
Martin Luther

Words of Wisdom

I've learned that fear limits you and your vision. It serves as blinders to what may
be just a few steps down the road for you. The journey is valuable, but believing in
your talents, your abilities, and your self-worth can empower you to walk down
an even brighter path. Transforming fear into freedom - how great is that?
Soledad O'Brien

Love is the master key that opens the gates of happiness, of hatred,
of jealousy, and most easily of all, the gate of fear.
Oliver Wendell Holmes, Sr.

Promises

As a boy, David showed great fearlessness. His secret can be found in Psalm 56:3-4;

> When I am afraid,
> I will trust in you.
> I praise God for what he has promised,
> I trust in God, so why should I be afraid.
> What can mere mortals do to me?

David admits in this Psalm that he wasn't totally void of fear. When he felt fearful, he relied on his past experiences with the lion and bear and placed his trust in God.

> There is no fear in love; but perfect love casts out fear,
> because fear involves punishment, and the one who fears is not perfected in love.
> 1 John 4:18

There is only one perfect love, and it is found in the source of all love. That source is God. When we fill our lives with His love, fear can no longer control us.

Refer to the last section of the book entitled Aha Moments.
We encourage you to record your personal lessons learned.

Prayer

Loving Father,

Give us the courage to address our fears and the wisdom to control them.
Fill us with your love and help us to begin to see the adventurous and fearless beings
you created us to be.
Amen

The UNSTUCK BLESSING

May your heart be filled with Thanksgiving

May your mind be driven by Courage

May your willingness to move forward

Bring you into a life filled with joy!

PART 2

Doubt

Definition

DOUBT is the feeling of uncertainty or lack of conviction.

Unstuck Viewpoint

Whenever troubles come your way, let it bring opportunity for joy. For when your faith is tested, your endurance has a chance to grow. So let it grow, for when your endurance is fully developed, you will be strong in character and ready for anything. If you need wisdom, if you want to know what God wants you to do, ask him and he will gladly tell you. He will not resent your asking. But when you ask him, be sure that you really expect him to answer, for a doubtful mind is as unsettled as a war of the sea that is driven and tossed by the wind...

STOP! HOLD ON! WAIT A MINUTE!!!!

Doesn't this sound like something your school counselor, principal or mother would have said?

Really? This can't be in the Bible!

It is! It's found in the Book of James which is a really small book toward the end of the Bible. This is one of those references that I once thought should be erased. Just scratch that one out, and put it in the pile of "doesn't pertain to current life." However, over decades of making jest of this scripture, I now see the wisdom in it.

STOP! HOLD ON! STAY WITH ME!!!

Anytime trouble comes our way, we have a choice. Do we choose to see the glass half empty or half full? Or do we say, "that's not my glass?" Difficult times are a part of life. How we deal with them shows our emotional maturity.

Some would say that if we don't react, we're just holding in our feelings. Others would claim that we should be peacemakers, which means we should look the other way when terrible things happen to us. Still, others would say that when bad things happen to us, it's somehow our fault and is payment for all the bad things we've done.

I see it as if we have two choices. When we are faced with negative circumstances, we can either add it to the list of reasons we feel victimized OR we can use it as an opportunity for personal growth. If you guessed the second option is the best, you are correct!

Being faced with tough choices, or consequences of our own actions, or consequences of other's actions, all qualify as 'trouble coming our way". The secret is to look at each of these as an opportunity to become stronger, wiser, bolder, softer, quieter, peaceful-er.

So, where does the joy come in? Joy comes way before the bad situation begins.
>It begins with us believing that God is with us and has promised to never leave us.
>It begins by allowing life's curve balls to make us stronger.

It begins with refusing to be the victim.

It begins by allowing ourselves to learn from the past instead of blaming it.

It begins when we accept that we are worthy of having good things happen to us.

It begins when we are willing to trust the Creator of the Universe.

When we look at life's troubles as a means of building our character, growing our endurance, making us stronger, they become a means of learning rather than a means of destroying us.

Is your glass half empty? Or is it half full?

I guarantee you that the group that is half full is always ready to say, "Pour me another one!"

> *My coming to faith did not start with a leap but rather a series of staggers from what seemed like one safe place to another. Like lily pads, round and green, these places summoned and then held me up while I grew. Each prepared me for the next leaf on which I would land, and in this way I moved across the swamp of doubt and fear.*
>
> *Anne Lamott*

A Personal Story from Anita

I didn't grow up reading the Bible. When friends would discuss scriptures or biblical stories, I'd pretend to know what they were talking about. I'd nod my head in agreement because I didn't want to appear uneducated. Without even reading the stories from the Bible myself, I had confidently come to my uninformed conclusion that there was no way the Bible could still be accurate. You could say that I was a doubting Thomas!

I convinced myself that the validity of the Bible was similar to the game of telephone that I played as a young girl. My friends and I would form a line, shoulder to shoulder, where the first person would whisper some gossip in their neighbor's ear. In turn, they relayed what I had originally said to the person at their side and so on down the line. The last person would shout out what they thought they heard through this grapevine. We'd double over with laughter at how the story had drastically changed as it made its way through each girl's imagination. Naively, I used this same logic on my doubting the validity of the Bible.

I began to study the Bible and how the stories correlated to documented records and centuries of research. I began to live by the morals and hopes as set forth in these scriptures that are rich in history and promises. I know now that to live without them would be a tragedy.

Two decades before I began my walk with the Lord, I visited the small village of Barra de Navidad. I didn't realize it at the time but it was there that I began my journey of faith.

Twenty five years before my visit, on September 1, 1971, Hurricane Lily passed over the town, where the residents fled their homes and took refuge inside the church of San Antonio. While they gathered and prayed, the arms of Jesus on the cross fell to his sides and the storm stopped. The local legend states that the arms of Jesus had held back the tides and spared the town from being destroyed.

The town's people directed me to the weathered Church of San Antonio, where I witnessed an enormous wooden cross hanging on the alter. On that cross was a paint-chipped plaster replica of Jesus Christ with both arms dangling by his side. It is said that God lowered Christ's arms to contain the storm and only He will raise them. I didn't doubt it.

Many years later, I visited several churches throughout the world; some primitive and some opulent but no matter what they looked like, each one depicted the undeniable story of Jesus Christ.

Do I still doubt? From time to time, I do. The difference now is that I ask questions, read scriptures and take time to listen; I am usually blown away by the clarity that I find.

Unstuck Viewpoint

We have a friend who is consistently reading the Bible and praying. From all outward appearances, she appears to be a woman of God. The pages of her Bible are worn. She says all the right things. She is a kind and generous person. She's got style, is healthy and attractive, and has a family that loves her.

Yet, she is still filled with fear, worry and stress. She finds problems where there are none. She worries about everything and doubts what's around every corner.

How can someone who claims to have so much faith still live in such fear and doubt?

Romans 8:28 is a very powerful and bold verse. It says:
And we know that God causes all things to work together for good...

This verse leaves me with three questions:
The first, do we believe? Do we really believe that God is causing all things to work for our good. The second question is: What is everything? And finally: What does "GOOD" look like?

Let's begin with the third question, What does "GOOD" look like? We would be mistaken if we defined Good as only material gain, great success, or popularity. We must also define Good as our benefit, growth, maturity or development.

The second question, What is everything? Some see God as a puppeteer who is pulling strings and making us dance. Some see Him (or Her) as a God who makes sure you have a parking spot next to the front door at Walmart. The emotionally mature would define everything as all of life's situations, whether they are good or difficult.

But it all comes down to the first question, *Do we believe?*

The Unstuck Translation looks like this:

> We know that God will work every situation in our life for our personal benefit.

> Or the simple version: Everything is always working out for me!

What would your life look like if you really believed this promise?

UNSTUCK CHALLENGE

Unlike Fear that needs to be overcome, Doubt simply needs to be replaced.

How do we do this?

By testing it.

In our story of David, King Saul suited David up in a warrior's uniform. David tried it on but removed it because, "He had not tested it." It's a wise man who test's theories before believing them to be true.

It's okay to test scriptures. It's okay to ask God to prove promises to be true.

In this challenge, we are going to do a little testing by imagining.
We are going to take Romans 8:28 literally. "God's working everything for your good".

"WHAT?" You are screaming.

Yep! Literally.

You only have two assignments:

    1. Repeat to yourself everyday, ALL DAY; "Everything is always working out for me."

    2. Then live each day as if you believe it! Everything IS working out for you.

David experienced God's protection when he killed the lion and the bear. David didn't need God to keep reminding him that He was with him. David experienced it firsthand and from then on, he did not doubt.

When we begin to experience life based on a belief that God is working everything for our good, we look at disappointment differently. We see failure as a step toward success. We begin to see the countless miracles happening all around us and for us because we are not living in doubt.

Record the amazing ways that 'Everything is always working out for you!' in Aha Moments.

Taking Action!

Journaling

"Everything is always working out for me."
Document the events as you begin living life
BELIEVING that God is working all things out for your good.

Can you Imagine?

Fearless Adventures

Now that we've become fearless adventurers, put on your goggles of faith and begin seeing life in a new way.

When doubt knocks at your door, don't answer. When uncertainty calls, hang-up. When worry creeps in, proclaim - "Everything is working out for me!"

Begin drinking from a full glass, you have nothing to lose.

Confessions

People who have overcome doubt exemplify self-confidence and courage. Circle the words you find in our word search on the next page that are good examples of portraying such qualities.

Do you possess any of these characteristics?

confident	nervy	anxious	interesting
hesitant	afraid	monotonous	scared
gutsy	agitated	spirited	unafraid
apprehensive	playful	nervous	thankful
serious	spiritless	smart	angry
shy	suspicious	positive	unexciting
frightened	strong	fun-loving	mad
tough	happy	dreary	tedious
bold	tense	dull	friendly
nervous	common	upset	enjoyable
curious	frightened	courageous	complainer
self-conscious	pleasant	sad	Godly
wise	sincere	close-minded	fearless
timid	sassy	daring	honest
uninteresting	panicky	negative	lost
discouraged	chicken	frantic	judgemental
awesome	sure	inspiring	assured
organized	unreliable	joyful open-	reliable
needy	disturbed	minded	drab
hot-headed	silly	controlling	adventurous
sheepish	exciting	unorganized	vengeful

Words of Wisdom

Faith and doubt cannot exist in the same mind at the same time,
for one will dispel the other.
Thomas S. Monson

Did you know...

It's interesting to note that the word Doubt is rarely found in the Old Testament. It is frequent in the New Testament. Before Christ, the Jews had the Law and placed their faith in it. They either obeyed or disobeyed. After Christ, the Christian life became about believing or doubting.

A Doubting Thomas is a skeptic who refuses to believe in anything without his or her own direct personal experience. This is in direct reference to the Apostle Thomas, who refused to believe that the resurrected Jesus Christ had risen and appeared to the other apostles. Until, of course, he could see it with his own eyes and feel the wounds on Jesus for himself.

Prayer

Loving Father,

Give us the courage to replace our doubt with an ever growing faith in your promises. Fill us with your love and help us to begin to see that you are working every situation out for our good. Let us begin to see the life of joy you have waiting for us.
Amen

The *UNSTUCK BLESSING*

May your heart be filled with Thanksgiving

May your mind be driven by Courage

May your willingness to move forward

Bring you into a life filled with joy!

PART 3
Courage

Definition:

COURAGE is bravery, valor, heroism, greatness of spirit in facing danger or difficulty. It is a universally admired attribute. From soldiers to entrepreneurs, writers to explorers, living with courage can help to define and build the life you want.

A Personal Story from Anita

Several years ago, my husband and I were making our way from the parking lot to the worship center at our Southern California mega-church. We rushed in and approached the steps at the same time as a beautifully dressed woman in her sixties. She shared with us that it was her very first time attending our church. We turned and in our haste said, "You will love it here" and kept on walking.

After we found our seats and gave a huge sigh of relief that we had made it on time, we realized that we should have done more. We asked ourselves, what were we afraid of? How hard would it have been to invite her to sit with us or show her to the sanctuary?

We looked around to make amends, but she was nowhere to be seen. That split second of opportunity was gone.

Were we so involved in getting to the church on time that we didn't leave any room in our hearts to reach out to others? We instinctively knew the answer and felt ashamed. Years later we moved to another community and began attending a much smaller church. We never forgot that woman. When the opportunity to become a host for Sunday services became available, we volunteered to become part of the greeting team. We knew that it wasn't too late to change and that God had long ago forgiven us, and it was time to forgive ourselves.

One very memorable rainy Sunday morning, my husband, Terry, slushed out to the parking lot with his extremely large umbrella and escorted a young man in his twenties from his car to the worship center. Terry asked him how he was doing, and he gave the traditional answer, "Fine".

Terry sensed he was not fine because of his red eyes and sad face so he asked him a second time. This time, Hector shared with Terry that he wasn't fine. Terry asked if he could pray with him and he accepted. They stood in the parking lot praying together in the rain. Once in the sanctuary, Terry asked me if we could change our seats and sit by him, which we did. After the service, we walked with him to the prayer team who embraced him with their prayers and their hearts. We said our goodbyes and didn't see him again for several months, often wondering what had become of him.

Then one Sunday, there he was! We were so happy to see him. He embraced us and told us about all the changes that took place in his life since we had last seen him and how wonderful his life had become. It was a joyous reunion.

At a recent Sunday service, our Pastor announced that Hector was killed in a motorcycle accident.

Opportunities may only show for a fleeting moment. Don't miss the signs. Throw your fears and negative self-talk out the window and have the courage to step out in faith. Take a chance on making a difference in someone else's life. It will fill your own with joy.

Unstuck Viewpoint

Mark Twain wrote, "With courage you will dare to take risks, have the strength to be compassionate and the wisdom to be humble. Courage is the foundation of integrity." Courage doesn't mean you are never afraid. Courage just means that you don't let fear stop you.

Fear is a serious issue that many people are dealing with on a daily basis. Sadly, many have allowed themselves to be obsessed by fear to the extent that it influences their whole life and future. It is an obstacle that can hold people back from having what God wants for them.

The words "Fear not" have been used throughout Scripture. It teaches us that God is with us and reminds us to let Him carry our burdens. As children of God, fear is something we have to control to be able to reach our full potential.

Do you have the courage to begin your journey to conquer your fears?

What do you think the first steps would be?

When you free yourself from fear, do you have something to replace it?

What might that be?

If fear has consumed your life, you will feel a loss when it's gone. You will also find that you'll have more time. What will you do with that time?

Be prepared to fill the gap; begin reading scriptures or taking the courageous risk to reach out and help others.

A Personal Story from Jeannie

2008 was a strange year for me. Both of our children were married that year. My husband's job offered the opportunity to move from our beloved condo in Chicago to a small beach town on the Central Coast of California.

Each of these monumental events would be placed high on the list of "life's most stressful situations". All three in one year had the potential to put one over the edge, and it did.

Planning weddings, selling a house, deciding on living arrangements on the other side of the country, saying good-bye to friends consumed my time. Closing one way of life and anticipating a new one was exciting; it was a new beginning for everyone, the next phase of all our lives. However, somewhere between excitement and anticipation, Fear snuck in and invited Anxiety to join in.

I experienced panic like never before. Every day was a struggle. At times, I felt I was losing control of my own mind. My thoughts were no longer my thoughts, rather they were consumed with Fear. I knew that this wasn't how I wanted to live, that I had to figure out how to get Fear under control and get my life back.

When 2009 arrived, we were on the other side of two weddings and a move across the country. In the decision to make the move, I had given up my job believing that I would find another opportunity. Add career change to the list of stressful events.

I had been in the coffee business for most of my adult life. I loved it. I never wanted to do anything else but train managers, share my knowledge of the little brown bean, and drink coffee. I accepted a manager's position with Starbucks. I was once again just managing one store.

At the beginning of 2010, I had been noticing that besides the energy it took to overcome the constant presence of Fear, I was feeling as if I had aged 100 years. I was out of breath most of the time and even the simplest tasks wore me out. One Friday afternoon, my husband picked me up from work. It was all that I could do to say, "take me to the ER, I can't breath".
It was determined that I was having a severe allergic reaction to something. A few weeks later it was discovered that something had a name; it was coffee!

In two short years, everything I loved, everything I did, everything that I had worked for had changed, and now the career that I had found so much passion in had been taken away.

Living a life allergic to something so prevalent as coffee is almost impossible. Restaurants, stores, offices, airplanes, airports, grocery stores, friends homes, church, there's not many places in the world coffee isn't served, brewed or sold. Fear took every advantage of this new situation, and I spent the next few years safe in my house. When I ventured out, the EPI pen and inhaler were always close at hand.

Fast forward to the present. I am on the other side. It took all my strength, but Fear no longer controls me. Oh, it tries, but I've learned to get it back in his cage quickly. Anxiety plays with my emotions, but it, too, knows it has no hold on my life.

As for coffee, I found a chiropractor who worked his magic, and I can once again smell the amazing aroma of coffee without fearing for my life.

What does this have to do with Courage? *Everything!*

For those who are struggling, fearful, anxiety driven, who feel trapped or stuck,

Courage is what is required to begin moving forward.

Courage pushes us out of our comfort zones and into new possibilities.

Courage walks along side us, arm in arm, through every valley and over every mountain.

Courage supports us when life falls apart.

Courage wakes us up each morning when all we want is to sleep the day away.

Courage allows us to get Fear and Doubt under control.

Courage takes us from stuck to Unstuck.

Courage keeps us breathing when our breath has been taken away.

UNSTUCK CHALLENGE

In this chapter we've discussed Fear, Doubt, Faith and Courage.

What keeps you continuing to choose Fear over Faith?

Do you want to live the life that God wants for you?

Are you ready to get UNSTUCK?

We've learned to put on our *Cape of Courage* and overcome fear by locating its beginnings. In doing so, it gives us a new perspective and allows us to change our reactions and responses.

We've imagined we believe "Everything is always working out for us," and we're learning to see life through *Goggles of Faith*.

David could have looked back at the time when the lion and bear attacked his flock with a different perspective. He could have been angry that 'God allowed' such a thing to happen. He could have been fearful that such an attack would happen again and never conquered the giant.

But David chose to see God's protection.

The final challenge is to take some time and look back over your life. This time, you are not looking for fear's conception, rather God's protection. What events could be your very own Lion and Bear stories?

Write a new story seen through the *Goggles of Faith*. Next, begin to tell that new story. The story that involves you and a God that has your back and has been there all along. In telling this story, you'll never be stuck again.

Taking Action!

Journaling

As you look back over your life, ask God to give you David's eyes. Look back over situations that changed the course of your life and find where God's hand was there to protect and guide. If you can't see it, ask God to show you.

You're not looking for those events that had a fairytale ending. Rarely does life offer such experiences. When you begin to see life through David's eyes, you won't want the fairytales any longer. You're looking at the day to day, unexpected, potentially dangerous experiences that you have lived through.

Can you now see where God was protecting you?

Can you see God's provision?

Can you see the wisdom that you now have because of that experience?

Can you see David's God who was there all the time?

If so, write it down. Write your story from a new vantage point. Record it in a new light.

Can you Imagine?

We have imagined that we are Fearless Adventurers. We have pretended that we believe "Everything is working out for us." Now it's time to live it! UNSTUCK!!

Confessions

Who do you want to be? What characteristics do you want to be remembered for? Circle the words on the following page that are examples of qualities you want to possess.

confident	nervy	anxious	interesting
hesitant	afraid	monotonous	scared
gutsy	agitated	spirited	unafraid
apprehensive	playful	nervous	thankful
serious	spiritless	smart	angry
shy	suspicious	positive	unexciting
frightened	strong	fun-loving	mad
tough	happy	dreary	tedious
bold	tense	dull	friendly
nervous	common	upset	enjoyable
curious	frightened	courageous	complainer
self-conscious	pleasant	sad	Godly
wise	sincere	close-minded	fearless
timid	sassy	daring	honest
uninteresting	panicky	negative	lost
discouraged	chicken	frantic	judgemental
awesome	sure	inspiring	assured
organized	unreliable	joyful open-	reliable
needy	disturbed	minded	drab
hot-headed	silly	controlling	adventurous
sheepish	exciting	unorganized	vengeful

Words of Wisdom

We gain strength, courage and confidence by each experience in which we really stop to look fear in the face...we must do that which we think we cannot.
Eleanor Roosevelt

Courage is resistance to fear, mastery of fear, not absence of fear.
Mark Twain

Promises

They do not fear bad news;
they confidently trust the Lord to care for them.
They are confident and fearless
and can face their foes triumphantly.
Psalm 112:1, 7-8

Be strong and of good courage, do not fear nor be afraid of them;
for the LORD your God,
He is the One who goes with you. He will not leave you nor forsake you.
Deuteronomy 31:6

The LORD is my light and my salvation;
So why should I be afraid?
The LORD is my fortress, protecting me from danger.
So why should I tremble?
Psalm 27:1

Prayer

Faithful Father,

Give me the courage to control fear and resist doubt. Remind me daily that You are always working on my behalf. Thank you for your constant protection and guidance. Thank you for the life of joy that you offer each of us.
Amen

The *UNSTUCK BLESSING*

May your heart be filled with Thanksgiving

May your mind be driven by Courage

May your willingness to move forward

Bring you into a life filled with joy!

CHAPTER 2

GET OUT OF GOD'S WAY

Story from the Bible: Sarah and Hagar
Genesis 16-18

There is no story in the Bible that is a clearer example of effort vs. action than the story of Sarah and Hagar.

When Abraham was an old man, God promised him he would be the father of many nations. But when time passed and there was no child, his wife Sarah took matters into her own hands. Sarah had a lovely, young, Egyptian maid whose name was Hagar. Sarah convinced Abraham that since she was not successful in giving him a child, Hagar might be the solution.

Abraham and Hagar slept together with Sarah's full awareness and blessing. After all, it was Sarah's idea. And joy of joys, her plan worked. Hagar got pregnant.

Anyone else see how this has disaster written all over it?

Hagar realized the position that she was now in and Sarah felt the tension. This young woman is carrying the only child of Abraham, a man of great means and stature. In Hagar's mind, she had risen to the top, above Sarah.

Sarah was not happy and complained to Abraham about her situation. Abraham reminded her that Hagar's circumstance was a result of her own efforts. Then Sarah lashed out at Hagar, and Hagar makes a run for it.

A single, pregnant, Egyptian girl decided that living in the wilderness would be better than tolerating the anger of her mistress. From every vantage point, Hagar is used, abused, manipulated and the victim in this story. As she wandered alone in the wilderness, the Bible says an angel found her sitting by a spring of water.

God hadn't lost sight of Hagar. God was getting ready to work it all out for her good. The Angel instructed her to return to Sarah.

The Angel gave her a promise from God and tells her,

"You are having a baby and will name him Ishmael. I will greatly multiply your descendants so that there will be too many to count."

"This son of yours will be a wild donkey of a man. His hand will be against everyone and everyone's hand will be against him. He will live to the east of all his brothers."

Hagar has a new name for God, she calls Him "a God who sees".

A God who sees.

A God who sees when we are being mistreated.

A God who sees when others are taking advantage of us.

A God who sees our future and has promised to make our paths straight.

I love Hagar's innocence here; after all, she was still a child. Hagar returns to Sarah and when the time is due, gives birth to Ishmael, just as the Angel had said.

It's another 14 years before Sarah gives birth to her son, Isaac. Fourteen years didn't soften her; she still was jealous of Hagar. Abraham was disturbed by the friction, and again we see a God who sees. God instructs Abraham to send Hagar and the boy away.

God makes Abraham another promise; "I will make Ishmael a nation also, because he is your descendant." Abraham rose early in the morning and took bread and a skin of water and gave them to Hagar. He gave her the boy and sent them away. She departed and wandered in the wilderness.

Hagar is once again wandering in the wilderness, but this time she has her son with her. When her water supply ran out, she told Ishmael to rest under the shade of a bush and sits down away from him. She assumes they will both die soon, and she doesn't want to witness it.

But Hagar knows a God that sees. Once again, an Angel appears and says to her, "What is the matter with you, Hagar? Do not fear, for God has heard the voice of the lad where he is. Arise, lift up the lad, and hold him by the hand, for I will make a great nation of him."

Then God opened her eyes, and she saw a well of water. She went and filled the skin with water and gave Ishmael a drink.

With all the drama, conflict, and hatred in this story, one might ask, what does this have to do with effort vs. action?

Long before there was drama, conflict, and hatred, there was man and a woman and a promise from God. Instead of Sarah waiting on God, she took matters into her own hands. She came up with what she thought was a solution for "God's" problem. She put forth great effort in devising a plan instead of waiting for God's inspiration to act.

There already was an action required. This was not Jesus's birth, there would only be one immaculate conception. The act of sex was necessary for Sarah to conceive. That was the inspired act, all the other stuff that Sarah did was effort in order to make something happen.

And indeed, something did happen. If you follow the descendants of Ishmael, it will lead you to our current world. Isaac was the beginning of the Nation of Israel, Ishmael was the beginning of the Nation of Islam.

That's quite a legacy for a woman who couldn't wait for God to fulfill His promise. Out of her own effort, she took matters into her own hands.

PART I
Effort vs. Action

Definitions:

EFFORT is a determined attempt to work, strain, strive or force an issue or a circumstance.

ACTION is the process of doing something, typically to be deliberate in achieving an aim or a goal. An undertaking or goal which inspires activity.

A Personal Story from Jeannie

As a teen, my friends and I tubed down the Crystal River. It was a summertime favorite. We'd make the forty-five minute drive, park our cars in the gravel parking lot, pay our fee, get on a big green bus and be taken up the river.

We excitedly exited the bus and made our way to the river bank where giant black inner tubes were tossed in the water. Laughter and cheers would erupt as all who were watching ran into the rapids in hopes of catching a tube before it caught the current and floated on without us. Once a tube was captured, we'd jump on, wiggle our butts into the center, lay our heads back and float down the river. No paddles, no oars, we were swept away by the current.

Imagine for a moment, while we were on the tubes, we began paddling against the current. Or, if we had been dropped off down stream and expected to make our way upstream. That would have taken great EFFORT. Such an effort most likely would have created anxiety because we weren't getting anywhere. We would have been frustrated. By the end of the day, we would have felt as though we had failed. In contrast, allowing the current to guide us was relaxing, enjoyable and a peaceful journey.

I have come to understand that allowing God to guide us is just like allowing the current to carry us down the river. So the question is, in everyday life, how do we know when we're paddling upstream or allowing the current to guide us?

It's easier than we think! We know this by our emotions. When we are striving to make something happen, when we are exerting our own effort, we feel frustrated, anxious and the fear of failure haunts us. Learning to trust that God will provide a current to guide us creates joy, excitement and peace.

Unstuck Viewpoint

EFFORT is different than action. Typically, when we are putting forth EFFORT, we are paddling up stream. We are working really hard and going nowhere. There's a huge difference between floating down the river and paddling up it.

ACTION is never an effort. Action comes out of motivation and inspiration, not out of obligation.

You have an idea, you think it through. You begin to develop a plan; you ponder and explore your options. When you feel this is something worth pursuing, you have a choice: Either you believe it's all up to you to make it happen (effort); or, you wait and watch with great anticipation. When opportunity makes itself known, you spring into action, which will never feel like effort!

When we work out of EFFORT, rarely do the results equal the time and energy we've invested. There is usually a cost; this can be relationships, financial, stress or even our health. Effort equals work.

Personal Perspective

Do you live with the pressure that life is only going to happen if YOU make it happen?

Have you ever attempted something and felt as though you were only finding dead-ends?

Do you feel guilty or angry when a plan doesn't work?

Now, think back to a situation where you can see where you took matters into your own hands.

What were the results?

What was the cost?

What was the motivation behind the need to put forth the effort?

A Personal Story from Anita

Several years ago, my husband and I decided to pray together, aloud each evening before we went to bed. Before that decision was made, I had thought praying was personal. I only spoke to God in my head. I had never really prayed aloud before and didn't even know how to start. Terry gave me some words on how to begin and how to finish, but he said the rest was up to me.

Well, I got pretty good at it. My prayers went on for so long that he'd have to stop me or we'd never get to sleep. Then, I began to talk to God all day. I didn't even realize when it happened, but God became my best friend and confidant. He is always with me now. When a decision has to be made, it is a no-brainer, I simply ask God to show me the way.

As a result, when a job opportunity presented itself to my husband, we didn't rush into a decision as we would have in the past. We prayed for God's guidance and waited. We didn't force the issue, we waited and watched and God didn't disappoint. He showed us time after time, sign after sign, that Terry should take the new job.

At first we didn't recognize the signs, but they were there. A phone call here, a comment there, a question asked, a question answered or unanswered. Once we realized that these were not coincidental actions, my husband gave his resignation and accepted the new position. It was the easiest decision we ever made because we didn't make it alone, or did we make it at all?

It was effortless!

UNSTUCK CHALLENGE

The stories of David and Sarah parallel as both experienced God's protection and provision. Yet, even though Sarah had a direct promise from God, Sarah got in the way. She took matters into her own hands. The result was frustration, anger, resentment, fear and anxiety. David, on the other hand, didn't forget what God had done and was able to overpower Goliath.

This Unstuck Challenge is one of observation.

Be mindful of your emotions. Pay attention when you move from Effort to Action. Feel the emotional shift within you.

Effort brings with it pressure, anxiety, fear, inadequacy, self-doubt, and insecurity. It will drain you of your time, energy, resources, and emotions.

Action brings with it inspiration, motivation, fulfillment, accomplishment, and security. It will restore your time, energy, and resources. It will energize you.

Get in tune with your emotions during this challenge. A good test to see if you are working out of effort or action is to monitor your time, energy and resources.

Taking Action!

Journaling

Write about the times in your life you know you took matters into your own hands.

What were the results?

What was the cost?

What was the motivation behind the need to put forth the effort?

Compare these times to when you felt inspired. How did they differ?

Woulda, Coulda, Shoulda

Make a list of your current Hopes and Dreams and prioritize them.

Walk in my Shoes

Transport yourself into the story of Abraham, Sarah, and Hagar.

Which character do you relate to?

Abraham who waited patiently for God to fulfill his promise.

Sarah who was impatient with God and took matters into her own hands.

Hagar who became the victim.

Words of Wisdom

"Never mistake motion for action."
Ernest Hemingway

"Don't judge each day by the harvest that you reap but by the seeds that you plant."
Robert Louis Stevenson

Promises

Cease striving and know that I am God.
Psalm 46:10

Better to have one handful with quietness
than two handfuls with hard work
and chasing the wind.
Ecclesiastes 4:6

Prayer

Gracious Father,

Remind me that you are working in my life.
Nudge me when I forget to let you lead.
Give me patience to wait for your direction.
Amen

The UNSTUCK BLESSING

May your heart be filled with Thanksgiving

May your mind be driven by Courage

May your willingness to move forward

Bring you into a life filled with joy!

PART 2
Easy vs. Lazy

Definition:

Easy is achieving without great effort; presenting few difficulties.
Lazy is an unwillingness to work or use energy.

A Personal Story from Jeannie

Anita and I are doers. We've both had success in our careers and relationships. We dream big and live very full lives. We are confident in our abilities and when faced with an opportunity, we most likely will say, "Sure, we can do that!"

For most of my life, I lived in the world of Effort. I would get an idea and as soon as the excitement over the possibility passed, I'd be filled with anxiety, fear, and pressure that it was up to me to make it happen. Many times I succeeded, but most of the road to success was not fun or enjoyable. This was far from living the Easy Life.

In recent years, I've discovered this idea of putting Effort aside and allowing myself to wait for the inspiration to take Action. Now, if you are a doer such as I am, you are most likely asking, "What do you mean, DO NOTHING? You can't sit on your sofa and be successful! Lazy people sit around waiting for big things to happen."

I said these very words most of my life; and on some level, they are correct.

However, sitting on your sofa can be a big part of being successful and living the Easy Life.

The Easy Life or the Life of ACTION goes something like this: You get an idea. You love this idea. You know down deep in your gut that this is an idea that will work. Your next step...sit on your sofa and wait! Go to the beach and watch the waves. Take a hike. You wait! Wait until an opportunity crosses your path. When it does - you take action.

When I decided to try this Easy Life idea, I was blown away by the opportunities that crossed my path. I didn't have to go looking for them. I didn't need to brainstorm. I didn't need to sell anyone on my ideas or manipulate anyone into supporting them. One by one, pieces of the puzzle would fall into place. What was required of me? To wait, watch, and be ready.

My life is far from Lazy. I am busier now then I ever have been. I am more involved then ever before. I am seeing greater success than in the past. Most of all, I have more free time to be lazy. It's bizarre, as if I'm living at times in an alternate universe. Tasks that once took days seem to get finished in hours. Daunting tasks get picked up by someone more capable than me. Life is exciting, fun, adventurous, and best of all, peaceful.

When I get an idea now, I allow the excitement and anticipation to drench me. I breathe deeply and am grateful that inspiration has given me this particular idea. My next thought? I should go to the beach.... and I do!

I've learned that if I watch and wait, the new big black inner tube that I've just jumped on will begin floating downstream and bump into others who are riding the same current. We will end around the bend where God has something amazing waiting for us. When we finally arrive, we will be rested, relaxed, energized, and grateful.

Unstuck Viewpoint

I have one of those big red easy buttons from Staples on my desk. When pressed, a deep male voice says, "That was easy!" This particular model has the ability to say "that was easy" in over twenty languages. I bought one for my co-worker. We use this button all the time. Mine speaks in English, he's learning twenty languages, which to be honest doesn't feel very easy.

Looking for the easy way is not necessarily looking for the lazy way, there is a difference.

Ever walked into someone's home and had to forge a path through piles of clothes, papers, boxes, and toys? Ever open a closet door and felt the need to put your hand up in order to protect yourself from falling objects? Got a junk drawer? Got a junk room? Ever talked with someone who took ten minutes explaining all the reasons why they didn't finish a task when finishing the task would have only taken five?

I'm all about easy, keep it simple! Keep it light! Laziness is Easy's evil cousin. Easy saves time, Lazy wastes it.

Taking an afternoon to organize and simplify your office will save you time in the future. Keeping your house tidy saves time when you go to clean. Cleaning out the junk drawer makes it easier to find the junk you need. Nike would say, "Just Do It!"

Anita's Favorite Fisherman Story

Jeb the fisherman spent most of his mornings sitting by the sandy shore of the sea with his line in the water. He loved the sun on his skin and smell of the ocean. His eyes squinted from the noonday sun. Tied to his rickety chair was a rope that ran down the sand into the water. Attached to the cord was a burlap bag filled with twenty-four Atlantic Croakers.

"One more to go", Jeb would say to himself, "and I'll have my limit for the day". He pulled out his pocket watch. "Twelve noon, Maria should be putting lunch on the table about now." Oh, how he looked forward to his afternoon siesta with his wife by his side.

"Hey, Old Man," called the stranger walking down the beach. "Catch anything?"

"I did!" Jeb's eyes twinkled with delight as he reeled in the last fish of the day and began to pull on the rope to retrieve his catch. "Want to see 'em?"

"You bet," said the stranger.

Jeb tugged on the thick twine and produced a bag bursting with fish.

"Whoa! I've never seen so many fish in my life! You're the best fisherman I ever saw," he said. "You know what you should do? You could start your own fishing business. You can buy a boat, no, you could buy a fleet of boats and hire half the town... can you imagine how many fish you could catch then?"

Jeb scratched his head and asked, "Then what?"

"Well, if you work really hard, you'd probably be able to sell your fish and make lots of money."

Jeb lifted the bag of fish into his wagon and smirked, "Then what?"

"Geez, in ten years or so, you could sell your business, take all your money and retire. You want to retire don't you? If you retire you can do anything you want. What would you want to do old man?"

Jeb replied, "Sit on the beach and Fish!"

The stranger had a plan of great "EFFORT" to achieve the "ACTION" that Jeb was already enjoying.

UNSTUCK CHALLENGE

Isaiah 45:2a says, "I will go before you and make the rough places smooth."

There are those who would say that the path of least resistance is the lazy way. But, it is reasonable to believe that the path of least resistance is the same path that God made smooth. Lazy paths lead to more work and wasted time. Easy paths save time, energy, and resources and give you a firsthand view of God's desire to make our paths straight.

There is nothing wrong with taking the easy path, in fact, the more you take it, the more you see God's hand in preparing it for you.

Psalm 46:10a says, "Be still and know that I am God..."

Translation:
>   Be still and Know!
>   Know that I am God.
>   Know that I have gone before you!
>   Know that I am with you always!
>   Know that I will make your path straight.

Sarah had a direct promise from God. Yet, she found it impossible to wait and took matters into her own hands. The Unstuck Challenge for this lesson is learning to wait.

Set aside ten minutes each day to sit quietly to calm your mind. No music, no reading, no entertainment. Just ten minutes each day.

Taking Action!

Journaling

The stranger in our fishing story seemed to have a lot of fuel in his Effort, but he wasn't driving anywhere. The fisherman, on the other hand, seemed to have a destination in mind. Even before he got on the road, he was taking action.

Write about a time when after all your effort, you found yourself at the same place you started.

Describe a time when you found yourself saying, "That was too easy!"

Have you ever felt guilty when something came to you easily?

If so, where did the idea come from that makes you feel, if it isn't hard it isn't worth it?

Describe a time when you were lazy. What was the outcome?

What did you learn from answering these questions?

Woulda, Coulda, Shoulda

If you could wave your magic wand and change your life, what would be the first five things you would change?

Walk in my Shoes

In the last lesson, we compared ourselves to Abraham, Sarah, and Hagar. Take some time to write down your description of each of these characters, their traits, and personalities.

Promises

Take my yoke upon you.
Let me teach you, because I am humble and gentle at heart,
and you will find rest for your souls.
Matthew 11:29

I will go before you and make the rough places smooth.
Isaiah 45:2

Trust in the Lord with all your heart, and do not lean on your own understanding.
In all your ways acknowledge Him, and He will make your paths straight.
Proverbs 3:5-6

Prayer

Gracious Father,

Help me to see your hand working in my life.
Remind me daily that you have made a path for me. Give me wisdom to stay on your
path. Teach me to be still and listen for your inspiration.
Amen

The UNSTUCK BLESSING

May your heart be filled with Thanksgiving

May your mind be driven by Courage

May your willingness to move forward

Bring you into a life filled with joy!

PART 3

The Unleavened Life

Definition:

Unleavened (of bread) is made without yeast or other leavening agent.

In the Bible, the Israelites were instructed to eat only unleavened bread every year during Passover as a commemoration of their Exodus from Egyptian bondage. Since the children of Israel left Egypt hastily, they didn't have time for the bread to rise. So, on the first Passover, the bread was made without leaven or yeast. In Jewish homes, to this day the Passover celebration includes unleavened bread or matzoh which in Hebrew means bread or cake without leaven. For the full story of Passover, read Exodus 11 & 12:1-12.

A Personal Story from Jeannie

Our family celebrates Passover each year. We do it for a couple of reasons; one is that we are part Jewish, or at least hope we are. The other is that we love the deep heritage that comes with the Jewish culture.

I love this tradition. Over the years, we've acquired an ever growing circle of friends and family who join us at this celebration. We clear the living room of all unnecessary furnishings. We replace them with long tables and chairs in an attempt to share this meal with as many as we can possibly fit into our home.

Although I love the entire process, there is a particular point during the seder meal that touches me deeply. It's when we explain the purpose of the Matzoh bread. Matzoh is similar to a big flat cracker.

The simple Jewish translation goes like this: The Jewish people were waiting for God to free them from Egypt. They were so ready! They knew for certain that it was going to happen; so certain, in fact, that they didn't put any rising agents in their dough BECAUSE when God said 'GO!' they couldn't wait for their bread to rise. Thus, they ended up with a big flat cracker called Matzoh.

Life is so like bread. The more complicated the recipe, the more ingredients it needs, the longer it takes to make, to rise, and to bake.

When we live complicated lives, we miss so many opportunities. We wish we would be called to do great things, but if the call came, we'd have to let it go to voice mail and retrieve it when we had a minute to breathe, or perhaps next week.

It takes all of our energy to manage our responsibilities, debts, belongings, and relationships. It's exhausting. It's exhausting listening to people complain about their busy lives. Busy lives take all our time, energy, and attention.

There are amazing opportunities that cross our paths daily, but when we are overly busy, we become too preoccupied to see them.

An unleavened life is an Easy Life. It allows one to answer the call. Go when needed and grab an opportunity when it appears. An uncomplicated life gives us time to appreciate the world around us and the freedom to enjoy the pleasures of life.

When the time is right and God says 'Go!' or "Now!' or 'Here it is, just what you were waiting for!' - those living an unleavened life are ready, willing, and able.

The unleavened life is like a big flat cracker that goes anywhere you wish to go.

Unstuck Viewpoint

In this chapter, we've talked about the difference between Effort and Action. What separates those who choose easy over those who are lazy. And finally, living the Unleavened Life.

We've learned that it's our emotions that can assist in guiding us. When we feel anxiety, fear, frustration, and anger, our emotions are giving us warning signals that we are making it too difficult. That we may have missed the path of least resistance and are forging a path of our own.

If it becomes too challenging for us to stop, wait, breathe, we may have to dig a bit deeper and ask ourselves why?

> Why do we feel the need to succeed?
>
> Why do we feel that if we don't do it, no one will?
>
> What or where is our motivation coming from?
>
> Are we trying to prove that we matter?
>
> Are we trying to overcome past experiences?
>
> Are we fighting back? Or trying to get the world to notice that we are here?

What motivates us is important to understand. Once understood, we have the power to correct or heal past experiences allowing us to move forward with freedom.

Here are some questions to ponder. In doing so, you may gain insight into what motivates you. There are no right or wrong answers.

When facing challenges, do you feel the only way to succeed is to push through?

What does 'waiting on God' look like to you?

Are you spontaneous?

If not, why? If so, how does being spontaneous effect your day to day life?

Are you someone who needs a plan? If so, are your plans flexible?

What effect does it have on you when a plan isn't working out?

Do you like surprises? Why or why not?

When walking into unfamiliar territory, do you forge through

ignoring the danger signs

 or proceed with caution, barely moving forward? Why?

Do you make lists?

If so, how does it make you feel to check off your accomplishments?

Are you overwhelmed with the amount of responsibilities you have?

If so, why do you feel the need to take so much on?

Do you feel there just isn't enough time in the day, every day?

What makes it difficult to manage your time?

Do you base your decision making on 'not wanting to hurt someones feelings'?

Do you know it is an art to say NO? Can you say it?

Do you miss opportunities because you've over-scheduled?

Do you say "yes" to the best and "no" to the rest?

Too many responsibilities or belongings is a sign that we are out of line with what our life was meant to be. There is nothing wrong with having wealth or great material possessions, UNLESS they are robbing us of our time, energy, and resources.

The unleavened life is the Easy Button life. It's the path of least resistance. It's the life that says, "Here I am God, send me."

UNSTUCK CHALLENGE

If God presented you with an amazing opportunity, how quickly could you be ready to go?

God created the universe to operate on a twenty-four hour cycle. If there isn't enough time in the day to get everything done, either God messed up or you've taken on too much. I'm guessing it's you.

Commit to un-leavening your life by changing one aspect at a time. You can't change everything today so don't add extra leaven to your life by thinking you can.

Below is a recipe to help un-leaven parts of our life. Choose one, and only one and then begin the process. Once you have mastered the first area, then go on to the next. By doing one at a time, you will develop new habits that you can use for the rest of your life.

Unleavened Life Recipe

BEGIN WITH YOUR SCHEDULE

Are you filling your time with unimportant events? Stop.

Fill in your calendar this way:

First fill in your commitments, got too many? Get rid of some.

Second, make time for your relationships. If you can't find time for relationships, you'll need to get rid of a few more commitments.

Third, schedule time for you. (This should be at the top of your list, but we expect that this is a new concept for you, so we'll ease you into it.) No time for you? Get rid of a few more commitments and possibly some relationships.

There are twenty-four hours in a day. You sleep 8, you work 8, you get dressed, eat, drive to work, drive home, which probably takes up another 4; that's 20 hours, only 4 hours remain. You have to use them wisely. Sometimes wisely is sitting on the porch with your husband or wife or making cookies with your kids. Wisely doesn't mean busy.

NEXT, UNLEAVEN YOUR BELONGINGS

If you haven't used it in 6 months, get rid of it.

If you can't remember the last time you wore it, give it away to

someone who needs it.

Holding on for "some day"? Why? When 'some day' comes,

you'll have a better idea.

The less you have to take care of, the more time you have for

doing what you love.

The Israelites knew God was going to free them. They were ready. We need to be ready, too.

What an amazing declaration Isaiah made when he said, "God, here am I, send me!" An unleavened life allows us abundant opportunities that can be missed when we're too busy, too tired, overcommitted or living lives that are overly complicated.

Let's un-complicate our lives. Prepare our unleavened bread and be ready for all the adventures God has in store for us.

Taking Action!

Journaling

Write about times when you missed opportunities because you were over-scheduled, overbooked, or overwhelmed.

Walk in my Shoes

Think about the role of each of our three main characters; Abraham, Sarah, and Hagar. Like them, have you ever hastily taken matters into your own hands without thinking about the consequences? Did it negatively affect your life?

Woulda, Coulda, Shoulda

What area of your life needs the most un-leavening? What steps can you take to begin the process?

Words of Wisdom

"We are all faced with a series of great opportunities brilliantly disguised
as impossible situations."
Chuck Swindoll

"Let God's promises shine on your problems."
Corrie Ten Boom

Promises

And He said to His disciples, "For this reason I say to you, do not worry
about your life, as to what you will eat; nor for your body, as to what you will
put on. For life is more than food, and the body more than clothing.

Consider the ravens, for they neither sow nor reap; they have no storeroom nor
barn, and yet God feeds them; how much more valuable you are than the birds!
And which of you by worrying can add a single hour to his life's span? If you
cannot do even a very little thing, why do you worry about other matters?

Consider the lilies, how they grow: they neither toil nor spin; but I tell you, not
even Solomon in all his glory clothed himself like one of these. But if God so
clothes the grass in the field, which is alive today and tomorrow is thrown into
the furnace, how much more will He clothe you? You men of little faith!

And do not seek what you will eat and what you will drink, and do not keep worrying.
For all these things the nations of the world eagerly seek; but your Father knows that
you need these things. But seek His kingdom, and these things will be added to you. Do
not be afraid, little flock, for your Father has chosen gladly to give you the kingdom.
Luke 12:22-32

Prayer

Gracious Father,

Give me the courage to Unleaven my life!
Amen

The UNSTUCK BLESSING

May your heart be filled with Thanksgiving

May your mind be driven by Courage

May your willingness to move forward

Bring you into a life filled with joy!

CHAPTER 3

ME, MYSELF, AND I

Story from the Bible: Cain and Abel
Genesis 4:1-16

Adam and Eve's firstborn son was Cain; he became a farmer. Their second son, Abel, became a shepherd.

The brothers made sacrifices to GOD, an expectation of that time. Cain brought to the LORD a gift from his farm produce. Abel brought several choice lambs from his flock. On this particular day, the LORD showed great favor to Abel and his offering but did not offer the same level of special acknowledgement to Cain. This made Cain very angry.

Cain was jealous of the favor that God had shown Abel on that day. "Why are you so angry?" The Lord asked, "Why do you look so dejected? Your jealousy has ignited your anger, and sin is waiting to attack and destroy you. You must control it!"

When God made this statement, He was focusing on Cain's response to His giving favor to his brother, not the quality of gifts that were offered.

Cain did not change his attitude and because of his jealousy, he took Abel into the fields and killed him, becoming the first recorded murder.

The LORD asked Cain, "Where is your brother? Where is Abel?" Cain lied to the Lord and said, "I am not his keeper."

God punished Cain with a life of wandering. Because Cain was not willing to change, he became a homeless fugitive and lived in fear that he, too, would be killed. Even in Cain's disobedience, however, God promised to protect him. The Lord put a mark on Cain to warn anyone harming him they would receive a sevenfold punishment.

This isn't a story that tells us that being a shepherd is good and being a farmer is bad. This isn't even a story of who gives the better gift to try to win God's favor. This is a story of attitude and graciousness. The Bible doesn't tell us why God showed favor on Abel, it just says that He did. The Lord told Cain he would be accepted if he responded in the 'right way.' Cain responded by killing his brother.

God gave Cain the opportunity to adjust his attitude, and he chose to be jealous and vengeful; as a result, sin was crouching at his door and Cain welcomed it. There was a clear choice that was available, but he made the wrong one.

How hard would it have been for Cain to have slapped Abel on the back with pride and be pleased with his success?

How do you feel when someone has more than you do? A better job, a bigger house or more talents? Are you supportive or would you secretly like to meet them in the field?

PART 1

Anger and Wrath

Definition:

ANGER and WRATH is an emotion that involves a strong, uncomfortable, and emotional response to a perceived affront, hurt or threat. Anger can occur when a person feels their personal boundaries or those of their loved ones are being or going to be violated.

WRATH in its purest form can also lead to violence and hatred.

A Personal Story from Jeannie

Have you ever worked or lived with someone who was very good at making bad decisions and you were the one left to clean up the mess? I have found myself in that very situation. A decision had been made at work not to confront someone whose actions were becoming destructive. Because of this decision, those who worked with him were continually cleaning up his mess. I was one of those cleaner-uppers.

I had countless conversations with myself about the situation and finally came up with a plan. I waited for the meeting to discuss the problem and repeated to myself, "God, keep me calm, give me wisdom. Don't let me get mad or overly emotional. Give me peace."

During my marathon prayer, I took a breath, looked up and these words unexpectedly came out of my mouth, "You will hold everyone accountable for their actions." I stopped and repeated it, "You will hold everyone accountable for their actions."

I recall the sky being blue with big white clouds floating by, "You will hold everyone accountable...," then I finished the sentence, "I don't have to!"

My entire life, I had told myself this very thing. I knew God will hold the wrong doers accountable, but to be honest, I never took it to heart. I thought I was here to make them accountable. I was here to point out the error of their way.

I never lived as if I truly believed God was in control of this part of life. I felt that I had to make everything right, fix all the broken, and demand justice when an injustice was being committed. It was a life-changing, aha moment, when I realized it wasn't up to me.

God will hold everyone accountable, for the good and bad, I DON'T HAVE TO!

The weight lifted, the pressure relieved; the responsibility of making others do what was right was no longer mine. If I trust that God is working everything out for my good, I can also trust that He will hold everyone accountable for the good and bad.

Most of my anger is caused because of others bad decisions that have negatively affected me. I've learned to be smarter about being in relationships with those who would practice such behavior. In those times, I can rest, be peaceful, be confident, that God has it covered. I need not waste my time, energy, or resources; that's God's job and He doesn't need my help.

A Personal Story from Anita

I was angry for two years and thought I was justified in my anger. In fact, I reveled in it. I spent many waking hours reliving the situation and rehashing the details. When I wasn't awake, I was dreaming of how I might remedy the situation even though it was out of my control.

My anger began recruiting judgment and resentment. I noticed that my sense of humor was waning, my jaw was tightening and my fun-loving disposition was becoming not so fun-loving. People started giving me advice about my obsession, which made me even more angry.

So how did I learn to forgive? Well, I started by reminding myself to pray; so I prayed. I picked up my Bible and found my answers in Scripture. I put all my trust in the Lord. My relief was immediate. I realized the only person I had been hurting was me.

> *Don't sin by letting anger gain control over you.*
> *Don't let the sun go down while you are still angry.*
> *Anger gives a mighty foothold to the Devil.*
> *Ephesians 4:26-27*

The Devil! I thought. I didn't do anything wrong, yet was I leaving room in my heart for the Devil to take hold. Had I been so filled with anger that I didn't even know the Devil was crouching at the door. A wrong had been done, and I was justified by being angry, right?

As I read the word of God, my heart began to soften and I began to feel a sense of peace. If God forgives, I thought, then who am I to continue to hold a grudge or be a judge? What made me think I could make that call?

When I got out of God's way and let my anger go, I was set free. I suddenly had more time on my hands and realized how much energy I was wasting by thinking, rehashing, and contemplating my situation. I had a choice to leave the door open with sin crouching at my door as Cain did, or fill my new found time with gratitude and graciousness.

You have heard that our ancestors were told, 'You must not murder.
If you commit murder, you are subject to judgment."
But I say, "if you are even angry with someone you are subject to judgment!
If you call someone an idiot, you are in danger of being brought before the court.
And if you curse someone, you are in danger of the fires of hell.
Matthew 5:21-22

UNSTUCK CHALLENGE

Most of us who have experienced anger can usually explain it as a result of what's happened to us or to someone dear to us. Anger can sometimes cause us to lose our ability to be objective even though we feel we have all the facts. Anger can take on physical and mental consequences.

What was it that made Cain so angry?

What did the Lord mean when he told Cain that he would be accepted if he responded in the right way?

If Cain would have controlled his anger and responded to the Lord, what do you think might have happened?

Uncontrolled anger can also negatively impact the people around us. Let's take a few moments to ask ourselves a few questions.

Have you ever been around an angry person?

Did you find it to be a challenge?

What emotions did they evoke in you?

Did you ever think you were impacting another person with your anger?

Now think of a situation when you were angry.

How long did it last?

If your anger hasn't ended, what are you waiting for?

What is the right amount of time to hold onto anger?

If you no longer feel anger, why did it end?

How did you feel after you let your anger go?

If you are still angry, decide how much longer you are going to burden yourself with these negative thoughts.

Jot down at the top of a piece of paper your age; at the bottom the age that you hope to live. Along the left side, number the years in between.

Now ask yourself, how may more of those precious years do you plan to be stuck angry at something or someone?

Make your decision; do you have a specific date that you plan to give up your anger? Or, do you plan to be angry for the rest of your life?

What is God asking you to do as a result of this study? Write a prayer responding to what you've learned. Below is an example to help get you started.

Dear Lord,
I forgive those that have hurt me or wronged me.
If You have forgiven them, then who am I to not forgive.
Please give me strength to turn my attention to You and not be the judge of others.
In Jesus name I pray.
Amen

Taking Action!

Journaling

Write down one situation in your life that makes you angry.

Then list:
>   all the reasons why it angers you.
>   all the ways it affects you.
>   why you feel so hurt by it.

Making a change

Read over what you have journaled. When you get to the end ask yourself, "What would it look like if I flipped the switch right now and turned my anger off?

Imagine doing it! Put your anger in a sack and drop it on the ground. Feel the freedom. Feel the peace. Imagining is the first step toward doing it.

When you've imagined long enough, you won't want to pick up that angry sack ever again.

Words of Wisdom

"People who fly into a rage always make a bad landing."
Will Rogers

*"Holding anger is a poison. It eats you from inside. We think that
hating is a weapon that attacks the person who harmed us. But hatred
is a curved blade. And the harm we do, we do to ourselves."*
Mitch Albom

"Hot heads and cold hearts never solved anything."
Billy Graham

Promises

Get rid of all bitterness, rage, anger, harsh words and slander as well as all
types of malicious behavior. Instead be kind to each other, tenderhearted,
forgiving one another, just as God through Christ has forgiven you.
Ephesians 4:31-32

Understand this, my dear brothers and sisters: You must all be
quick to listen, slow to speak, and slow to get angry. Human
anger does not produce the righteousness God desires.
James 1:19-20

Fools vent their anger, but the wise quietly hold it back.
Proverbs 29:11

Prayer

Forgiving Father,

Help me to release my anger and fill me with your love.
Amen

The UNSTUCK BLESSING

May your heart be filled with Thanksgiving

May your mind be driven by Courage

May your willingness to move forward

Bring you into a life filled with joy!

PART 2

Forgiveness

Definition:

FORGIVENESS is the intentional and voluntary process where a person undergoes a change in feelings and attitude regarding an offense, or perceived offense.

A Personal Story from Jeannie

Forgiveness is such an amazing gift. It doesn't matter if you are receiving forgiveness or asking to be forgiven, this is an action that frees us. Forgiveness is abundant, you'll never get to the bottom of the forgiveness barrel.

Forgiveness relieves us of guilt. It frees us of this heavy weight that so many of us find necessary to carry around. However, forgiveness rarely removes the consequences of the actions.

If you cut down a neighbor's tree, you can ask for forgiveness, but the tree is gone. If you break a valuable object you can ask forgiveness, but the object is still lost.

The wonderful thing about forgiveness is that I can offer it freely whether it's asked for or not. I don't need to wait for my offender to come to me on bended knee begging for forgiveness. I can freely offer it with or without their participation. Forgiving is an essential part of getting Unstuck.

There are times we aren't so willing to offer forgiveness, feeling as if we are owed something, and by holding on to un-forgiveness, the universe will line up and teach our offender a lesson and repay what has been stolen from us. It doesn't work that way.

Holding on to un-forgiveness is holding on to the wrong end of the stick. Un-forgiveness only hurts you and keeps you stuck in the muck of the past.

Life happens. Life gets hard. People take advantage. The first step in forgiveness is getting past the blame. When we live in a world of blame, we are allowing someone else to control and be responsible for our lives. In doing so, we become powerless. We become victims who are allowing the actions of others to determine our life's course and that is just about as stuck as one can get.

UNSTUCK CHALLENGE

Begin practicing the art of forgiving. Find one situation in your life that you've been unable to offer forgiveness. We suggest that you start small and work your way up. Decide that it's time to let it go, it's time to forgive and take a step forward.

Ask yourself:

> What is it about this situation that really bothers me?
> Am I afraid to offer forgiveness? Why?
> Do I feel in control over my offender by not forgiving them?
> What is the benefit of not offering them forgiveness?

Offering forgiveness does not have to be confrontational. In fact, there are situations where confronting your offender can do more damage. Offering forgiveness, letting go, releasing your anger or hatred can be done privately, between you and God.

Take your life back! Release others of the control they have over you. Forgive and begin to move forward in the amazing, wonderful, beautiful, exciting, creative, loving world that is waiting for you.

Taking Action!

Journaling

Create a "Forgiveness Journal". Tell about a situation where you were hurt or wronged. Name names! Get it all out on paper.

Write a forgiveness letter, forgiving them of every detail. Free yourself from holding on to the anger, resentment, and pain. Remember, the forgiveness barrel will never be empty.

Making a Change

Become an Ambassador of Forgiveness for one day. Keep the words, "I forgive you," on the tip of your tongue. Repeat it all day long. To the barista who messes up your latte, to the bank teller who is having an off day and makes you wait, to the driver who cuts you off, to the partner who assumes too much.

Get into the habit of offering forgiveness, it will free you from the imprisonment of the burden that you've been carrying.

Words of Wisdom

Forgiveness is an act of the will, and the will can function
regardless of the temperature of the heart.
Corrie ten Boom

Forgiveness is not an occasional act, it is a constant attitude.
Martin Luther King Jr.

Promises

You must make allowance for each other's faults and forgive the person who
offends you. Remember, the Lord forgave you so you must forgive others.
Colossians 3:13,

Don't speak evil against each other, my dear brothers and sisters. If you criticize each
other and condemn each other, then you are criticizing and condemning God's law.
But you are not a judge who can decide whether the law is right or wrong, your job is
to obey it. God alone, who made the law, can rightly judge among us. He alone has the
power to save or to destroy. So, what right do you have to condemn your neighbor.
James 4:11-12

Prayer

Loving God,

*Thank you for the gift of forgiveness. Help me to accept this forgiveness
for others and for myself. Teach me to generously offer forgiveness to all.
Amen*

The UNSTUCK BLESSING

May your heart be filled with Thanksgiving

May your mind be driven by Courage

May your willingness to move forward

Bring you into a life filled with joy!

PART 3

Learning to Trust

Definition:

TRUST is having the confidence, faith, and belief in the certainty, reliability, and truth of someone or something.

A Personal Story from Anita:

Although it was ions ago, I can still see my daddy leaning over the workbench in the garage as he assembled the go-cart for my brother and me. I kept him company while I practiced ballet barefoot on the cement floor; twirling my skinny little legs into a pirouette as the sweet smelling sawdust flew through the air. To this day, the feel of ice cold cement on the bottom of my feet evokes the safety of my childhood, my home, and my dad.

As a young girl, I felt safe and trusted everyone; I had no reason not to, after all, I knew my father would never fail me. He'd throw me high into the air, and I instinctively knew he'd catch me. I laid on my back in the deep end of the swimming pool, unable to swim and knew his hand under my back would keep me afloat. I peddled my bike without training wheels and sensed him holding the back of the seat until he knew I could balance alone.

Trusting came naturally then, but my life experiences have taught me to be more cautious as an adult.

I ask myself, when did trusting become so hard? Was it when I was a teenager and my dad and mom got divorced? Did my parents disappoint me even before that time? I can't pinpoint the date when perfection faltered and the realities of life triggered my skepticism.

Trusting other people and trusting myself is still difficult sometimes. But, when I trust in God, like I had trusted my father when I was a child, His love fills my heart with joy. It's unconditional and brings me peace.

A Personal Story from Jeannie

There's a relatively new sport called paddle-boarding. It requires two pieces of equipment, an oversized surfboard and a paddle. I recall the first time I saw a paddle-boarder, I watched in wonder, imagining what it must feel like to glide across the surface of the ocean. I concluded that it must be like walking on water.

Early one Saturday morning, my daughter, husband, and I ventured out to discover this new sport. Austyn, my daughter, was a pro the moment she got on the board. Jeff and I had a few more challenges.

You begin paddle-boarding on your knees. This is so appropriate because one is usually praying for God's safekeeping and that no sharks are currently visiting the area. You paddle out until you are safely away from docks or rocks. It is then time to stand. Jeff made the transition from kneeling to standing with little effort. And within a few minutes of pushing off, there were two paddle-boarders standing and one kneeling.

My first attempt took all the courage I could muster. I wobbled. I laughed. I envisioned myself falling into the cold ocean water. But I got up and my clothes were still dry. Within seconds of assuming this new position on an oversized surfboard, my legs began to quiver uncontrollably.

"I can't hold still!" I shouted out to my daughter.

"It's the waves," she replied.

"This has nothing to do with waves," I yelled back. "This is happening on top of the board, not underneath."

I allowed myself to quiver and quake for a few more moments until I plopped back down and finished the journey on my knees.

Our second time out, we were chatting with the owner of the rental shop as she was gearing us up.

"You did great the last time, right?" she asked.

"It was awesome," I replied. "I loved it!

"You got up ok?" She inquired while measuring two paddles against my height.

"No, but I don't mind staying on my knees, it's just so much fun," I said.

"Wait!" She said, looking at me as if I had just offended the paddle-boarding gods. "Tell me what happened."

"I stood up, but my knees and legs were trembling, and I couldn't get them to stop."

"Oh, that's easy," she said with a smile that forced me to believe her. "It's just muscle memory. You've never done this before, and your muscles and nerves don't know how to react, so they're going a little crazy.

"This is what we're going to do..." She retrieved a king-size paddle-board from the trailer, "You're going to take this one today. It's almost impossible to turn this one over, and it's going to give you a wider surface to stand on." She set the board on one end to demonstrate the size.

"When you get out there, you need to stand up repetitively five times; up and down, up and down. You have to teach your muscles how to react. After the fifth time, you'll have new muscle memory and you'll be on your way."

She was right! I paddled out on my knees and practiced standing. I looked like a paddle board Jack-in-the Box, but I didn't care because the last time I stood up, I was standing straight and tall. My legs had learned a new stance and I was standing strong.

Trust is very much like paddle-boarding. We've all had experiences in our life that give us good reasons not to trust, to keep our guard up, to build defenses. But, it is possible to create new experiences that teach our trembling and fearful selves to trust again, to stand straight and strong and feel as if we can walk on water.

Personal Perspective

On a scale of 1-10, 1 being lowest – 10 highest, where is your overall trust factor in your life:

Trusting strangers:

Trusting employer:

Trusting co-workers:

Trusting friends:

Trusting neighbors:

Trusting parents:

Trusting family members:

Trusting spouse/partner:

Trusting yourself:

Trusting God:

As you can see, there are many levels of trust.

Did any of your responses surprise you? Can you see a pattern?

When it comes to trusting God, was your trust high?

If not, why do you think that is?

Do you think if you knew Him better that you could trust him more?

When you rated the trust you have in yourself, were you perplexed by your answer? What might you do to strengthen the trust you have in yourself?

How do we trust ourselves when we are our biggest disappointment? When we have a track record of failures?

How do we trust a God that we've never seen, that we don't understand, quite possibly a God we aren't sure even exists?

I believe God is big enough that we can put Him to the test. I've done it many times, and each time God has proven himself to me.

A Personal Story from Jeannie

There was a difficult time in my life when things were rapidly changing, and people were making unwise decisions all around me. Those decisions were having an adverse affect on my life. Nothing was making any sense; it was out of control, as if I was living in an alternate universe.

Fortunately, I was reminded of three verses that I have heard all my life in what I proclaim to be my "Protective Shield".

The first verse is from Isaiah 45:2:

I will go before you and make the rough places smooth...

Which translated in my mind to this:

> *God has already gone ahead of us, He knows our futures, He has made a path that is easy.*

The second verse is Isaiah 54:17:

> No weapon formed against you will prosper.

Which translated as:

> *In our life, negative things are going to happen. They don't have to destroy us.*

And finally Romans 8:28:

> We know that God causes all things to work together for our good....

Translation:

> *Everything is always working out for us!*

We now refer to these three verses as the Unstuck Protective Shield.

Together they say:

> **God knows my future. In fact, He has already been there and while He was there, He cleared a path for me to follow.**

> **And even when bad things happen, He'll make sure they won't stick..**

> **Finally, "Everything is always working out for me."**

Those seven words make up the perfect sentence. "Everything is always working out for me." If we believed that statement we would approach life differently. We would see challenges as opportunities and would walk each day with an excitement and anticipation of all the wonderful things that are happening around us.

There is a fourth verse found in Jeremiah 29:11 which adds a shine and resilience to our shield:

I know the plans I have for you.
Plans to prosper you and not to harm you. Plans to give you hope and a future.

This is the new muscle memory that we want to create for ourselves. We must practice strengthening those muscles, so when we're caught off guard, we then have a shield that allows us to stand strong.

UNSTUCK CHALLENGE

When we begin evaluating our trust factors, it is very common to trigger past wounds and hurts. Some of these can be very painful.

God desires to heal those wounds and hurts. Our Protective Shield says, In our life negative things are going to happen. They don't have to destroy us. Everything is always working out for us! God is the only one who can take hurtful and scary situations and work them out for our good. But we have to be willing to give Him a chance. We have to be willing to rebuild our ability to trust.

God:
I don't know how to trust. The thought of it makes me sick to my stomach.
It makes my soul quiver, my hands shake, my heart beat faster, and my anxiety soar.

BUT I'm going to put my faith to the test. You said You have gone before me, that You know my future and You have made the way straight. You said, NO bad force will succeed against me. You said, EVERYTHING is always working out for me....

I want to trust You. I want to believe that it's true, but to be honest, it sounds too good and my life experience tells me differently. So I'm asking You to prove it.
Amen

What's your part of this? Shut up and watch! Put your mind in neutral, no excuses, no unreal expectations (a million dollars isn't going to show up), no anticipation. Just watch and keep your mouth closed. Continually remind yourself that "God is working everything out for me." You'll be amazed as you begin to see the miracles that are happening around you every day, all day.

Write down your miracles and watch how God is working everything out for your good.

God gave Cain the opportunity to change his heart and be different. He said no. God is always giving us an opportunity to change. He doesn't want us to stay stuck.

Taking Action!

Journaling

Create your "Everything is always working out for me" Journal.

Journal the adventures as you begin to see that everything is always working out for you.

Making a Change

Hold on tightly to the Unstuck Protective Shield and live like you believe it.

Isaiah 45:2: I will go before you and make the rough places smooth.

Isaiah 54:17: No weapon formed against you will prosper.

Romans 8:28: We know that God causes all things to work together for our good.

Words of Wisdom

The best way to find out if you can trust somebody is to trust them.
Ernest Hemingway

Promises

Trust in the Lord with all your heart and lean not into your own understanding.
In all your ways acknowledge Him and He will direct your path.
Proverbs 3:5-6

Prayer

Faithful God,

Teach me to trust again. Help me to find security in your promises. Nudge me when I get stuck. Show me the life of joy you intended for me.
Amen

The UNSTUCK BLESSING

May your heart be filled with Thanksgiving

May your mind be driven by Courage

May your willingness to move forward

Bring you into a life filled with joy!

The Final Act

Joyful

Definition:

Joy is the emotion of great delight or happiness caused by something exceptionally good or satisfying. A keen pleasure; elation in your heart. Showing or expressing joy, in your looks, actions or speech.

A Personal Story from Anita

What does it look like to have a joyful life? It looks like Delphine!

Delphine, my mother-in-law, exuded joy! You could see it in her eyes when she tended her garden, in her smile when her family entered the room, and in the way she embraced life in general. She was a God-loving, wheat farmer's daughter raised in North Dakota. She told delicious tales of adventures of her youth, loved to dance, and had a zest for life like no other. Her joy was contagious.

At 86 we took Delphine to the Gap to buy her size zero jeans. Her gait was a little slower than it used to be, and she walked stooped over from a lifetime of hard work. Yet, she was game for anything. A ride on a motorcycle behind her grandson or an exhilarating "Aha, do it again!" when her son drove 90 miles an hour with the wind in her face.

We entered the Gap like any other shopper. Delphine was giddy over the thought of her new jeans. Music was blaring from the intercom, which made it very difficult to hear or think. Before I even knew what happened, Delphine threw her purse on the counter and began to rock back and forth. She slowly lifted one leg and then the other. Her shoulders were bouncing, and her fists were moving up and down. She started swaying towards the elderly gentlemen at the next counter, who was also rocking back and forth with his hips jiggling, lips puckered, and arms raised high. The two approached each other like they'd been dancing together for years and time stood still.

The other patrons began to congregate. The clapping, whooping, and hollering brought my husband running from the dressing room half-dressed. He was overwhelmed with concern knowing his elderly mother was in the shop that had exploded into pandemonium in his absence, but was relieved when he saw the smirk on his mother's face.

When the music stopped, the gentleman resumed his purchase. Delphine brushed off her dress and picked up her purse. We paid, and she sauntered out of the store standing just a little bit taller.

That is what a joyful life looks like!

Get ready...yours is about to start!

The UNSTUCK BLESSING

May your heart be filled with Thanksgiving

May your mind be driven by Courage

May your willingness to move forward

Bring you into a life filled with joy!

Unstuck Commandments

1. Look at your past only to better understand your future.

2. Imagine a life of joy, Unstuck.

3. The 'Why Game' always ends with ME!

4. Fear can be your friend.

5. Have the Courage to be a Fearless Adventurer.

6. Look at life through the Goggles of Faith.

7. Make your efforts be few and your actions plentiful.

8. Easy is the path of least resistance.

9. The Unleavened life is the "HERE I AM GOD, SEND ME" life.

10. Leave anger, offer forgiveness, and learn to trust.

A final check!

It's time to measure how far we've come!

Circle the characteristic that describes the new UNSTUCK YOU!

confident	nervy	anxious	interesting
hesitant	afraid	monotonous	scared
gutsy	agitated	spirited	unafraid
apprehensive	playful	nervous	thankful
serious	spiritless	smart	angry
shy	suspicious	positive	unexciting
frightened	strong	fun-loving	mad
tough	happy	dreary	tedious
bold	tense	dull	friendly
nervous	common	upset	enjoyable
curious	frightened	courageous	complainer
self-conscious	pleasant	sad	Godly
wise	sincere	close-minded	fearless
timid	sassy	daring	honest
uninteresting	panicky	negative	lost
discouraged	chicken	frantic	judgemental
awesome	sure	inspiring	assured
organized	unreliable	joyful open-	reliable
needy	disturbed	minded	drab
hot-headed	silly	controlling	adventurous
sheepish	exciting	unorganized	vengeful

To those who have read our words
and have found the courage to move forward,
may your life be filled with joy...
UNSTUCK!

UNSTUCK TOOLS AND RULES

The Study Sections

This study is divided into three chapters, and each chapter is divided into three parts. Living "Unstuck" can be enjoyed as a daily study over several weeks or it can be explored at your own pace, according to your own personal schedule.

Taking Action!

We're going to get creative and use mental images in 'Can You Imagine' and 'The Why Game.' We'll bring back memories from our past in a lesson called 'Replay', and we'll talk to the kid in us in 'A letter from a Child.'

Below are the details and descriptions of these activities which you'll find in your workbook at the end of each chapter.

Can You Imagine

The concept of "Faking it till you make it" works for many of us, and if we are one of those who has been successful in faking it, we need to keep doing it.

Faking it can be a positive experience. But, it can also bring negativity that aides in keeping us stuck. To some, it might feel dishonest or that you're hiding something.

Many times, we're pretending to cover our hurt or the pain of disappointment for not achieving what or who we desire to be.

In Living Unstuck, we prefer practicing the art of pretending that we like to call '*Can you Imagine?*' When we pretend, we aren't being dishonest, and we aren't claiming a reality that doesn't exist. We use it to get into a new mindset, to focus in a different way, and to create situations that help us learn to grow through our imaginations.

Awhile back, I committed to pretend for a month that I was a very successful and prominent Author and Publisher. I'd walk into gatherings imagining how someone who had truly achieved success would walk. How would they interact? How would they carry themselves?

When faced with challenges, instead of moaning and groaning about them, I'd envision myself making smart decisions in order to create greater success. I put more thought into how I presented myself and what I chose to wear.

At the end of the month, the needle of success had barely moved, but the needle of my confidence, focus, clarity, and determination was off the chart. I was thinking differently. I was reacting in a new way. I was looking at life from a new vantage point, and I loved it!!

With each chapter, we offer a chance to imagine. We encourage you to do it in a way that would win you the Oscar. Use your imagination, tell your family what you're doing, and let them get involved. Open your imagination and create new worlds, new possibilities, and new opportunities. This is your fast track to getting Unstuck.

Games that Heal

We have all had life experiences that have affected us. When we experience trauma as a child, part of our emotional maturity may have been stunted. This is why when we achieve adulthood, we might still have childish behaviors. Some of our personality may never have matured with age.

There are some experiences that are too large for one person to handle. These are the times when we need to seek others who are trained and equipped to help us deal with those experiences.

We offer three exercises that can be very helpful in getting Unstuck when past experiences seem to have a hold on you.

The WHY Game

This one is easy, just keep asking yourself WHY after every one of your responses.
Example:
Why do I get so mad when he or she does that?

>   Answer: Because it makes me feel.....

Why does it make me feel.....

>   Answer: Because I hate when ......

Why does that bother you so much?

>   Answer: Because I feel like they think I'm a child.

Why do you feel like a child?

>   Answer: Because I don't feel important.

On and on you go until the answer comes back to you. When and only when the answer is about YOU, do you have any power to change it. And when you get the answer, you will feel powerful.

Replay

Let's pretend we are giants - wise and gentle looking down on a TV screen that is lying face up on the floor. We are watching a rerun of a past-life experience. We can fast forward, freeze frame, or rewind as often as we'd like. As we play the part of the giant, we will see the situation from a different set of eyes. In doing so, WE are able to provide commentary, insight, and an adult viewpoint to the situation. With this new perspective, we can begin the healing process.

I've done this several times, and each time as I reached the end of my rerun, the wise gentle giant brought clarity to the small hurting child in me. I could feel the healing begin immediately.

A Letter from a Child

This is a powerful exercise when dealing with situations from childhood. Begin by writing your own experience. To make it more effective, I recommend writing with the opposite hand using a pencil or crayon (a child's writing utensil). Write down everything; what happened, how you felt, and who was there. When it's all recorded, put down the crayon or pencil, fold the paper, and walk away.

After a short break, pick up the note and read it from an adult perspective. Separate yourself, this isn't your story anymore. It's a story of a child and you have the privilege to read it.

Once you've finished reading through the story, it is time for YOU, the adult, to respond. YOU will point out where adults may have responded incorrectly or where the child in the story should have been protected. Then YOU, the adult, can apologize and bring closure to your story.

You will be amazed how quickly wounds will heal, forgiveness will happen, and anger will diminish without the assistance of anyone else, just you and the kid.

Reference

Emotions - written by Barry & Robin Gibb, first recorded in 1978.

Jeremiah 29:11(NLT)

11 For I know the plans I have for you," says the Lord. "They are plans for good and not for disaster, to give you a future and a hope.

Story of David and Goliath 1 Samuel 17 & 18

Proverbs 3:24-26 (NLT)

24 You can go to bed without fear; you will lie down and sleep soundly.

25 You need not be afraid of sudden disaster or the destruction that comes upon the wicked,

26 for the Lord is your security. He will keep your foot from being caught in a trap.

Psalm 56:3-4 (NLT)

3 But when I am afraid, I will put my trust in you.

4 I praise God for what he has promised. I trust in God, so why should I be afraid?

   What can mere mortals do to me?

1 John 4:18 (NASB)

18 There is no fear in love; but perfect love casts out fear, because fear [a]involves punishment, and the one who fears is not perfected in love.

James 1: 2-6 (NLT)

Whenever troubles of any kind come your way, consider it an opportunity for great joy. 3 For you know that when your faith is tested, your endurance has a chance to grow. 4 So let it grow, for when your endurance is fully developed, you will be perfect and complete, needing nothing.

5 If you need wisdom, ask our generous God, and he will give it to you. He will not rebuke you for asking.6 But when you ask him, be sure that your faith is in God alone. Do not waiver, for a person with divided loyalty is as unsettled as a wave of the sea that is blown and tossed by the wind.

Psalm 112:1, 7-8 (NLT)

They do not fear bad news; they confidently trust the Lord to care for them. They are confident and fearless and can face their foes triumphantly.

Deuteronomy 31:6 (NLT)

6 So be strong and courageous! Do not be afraid and do not panic before them. For the Lord your God will personally go ahead of you. He will neither fail you nor abandon you."

Psalm 27 (NLT)

1 The Lord is my light and my salvation— so why should I be afraid?

The Lord is my fortress, protecting me from danger, so why should I tremble?

Story of Sarah and Hagar   7678Genesis 16-18

Psalm 46:10 (NASB)

10 "Cease striving and know that I am God;

I will be exalted among the [b]nations, I will be exalted in the earth."

Ecclesiastes 4:6 (NLT)

6 And yet,

"Better to have one handful with quietness than two handfuls with hard work and chasing the wind."

Isaiah 45:2a (NASB)

2 "I will go before you and make the rough places smooth;

Psalm 46:10a. (NLT)

Be still and know that I am God…

Proverbs 3:5-6 (NASB)

5 Trust in the Lord with all your heart

And do not lean on your own understanding.

6 In all your ways acknowledge Him,

And He will make your paths straight.

Luke 12:22-32 (NASB)

22 And He said to His disciples, "For this reason I say to you, [a]do not worry about your [b]life, as to what you will eat; nor for your body, as to what you will put on. 23 For life is more than food, and the body more than clothing.24 Consider the ravens, for they neither sow nor reap; they have no storeroom nor barn, and yet God feeds them; how much more valuable you are than the birds! 25 And which of you by worrying can add a single [c]hour to his [d]life's span? 26 If then you cannot do even a very little thing, why do you worry about other matters? 27 Consider the lilies, how they grow: they neither toil nor spin; but I tell you, not even Solomon in all his glory clothed himself like one of these. 28 But if God so clothes the grass in the field, which is alive today and tomorrow is thrown into the furnace, how much more will He clothe you? You men of little faith!29 And do not seek what you will eat and what

you will drink, and do not keep worrying. 30 For [e]all these things the nations of the world eagerly seek; but your Father knows that you need these things. 31 But seek His kingdom, and these things will be added to you. 32 Do not be afraid, little flock, for your Father has chosen gladly to give you the kingdom.

Story of Cain & Able Genesis 4:1-16

Ephesians 4:26-27 (NLT)
26 And "don't sin by letting anger control you."[a] Don't let the sun go down while you are still angry, 27 for anger gives a foothold to the devil.

Matthew 5:21-22 (NLT)
21 "You have heard that our ancestors were told, 'You must not murder. If you commit murder, you are subject to judgment.'[a]22 But I say, if you are even angry with someone,[b] you are subject to judgment! If you call someone an idiot,[c] you are in danger of being brought before the court. And if you curse someone,[d] you are in danger of the fires of hell.[e]

Ephesians 4:31-32 (NLT)
31 Get rid of all bitterness, rage, anger, harsh words, and slander, as well as all types of evil behavior.32 Instead, be kind to each other, tenderhearted, forgiving one another, just as God through Christ has forgiven you.

James 1:19-20 (NLT)
19 Understand this, my dear brothers and sisters: You must all be quick to listen, slow to speak, and slow to get angry.20 Human anger[a] does not produce the righteousness[b] God desires.

Proverbs 29:11 (NLT)
11 Fools vent their anger, but the wise quietly hold it back.

Colossians 3:13 (NLT)
13 Make allowance for each other's faults, and forgive anyone who offends you. Remember, the Lord forgave you, so you must forgive others.

James 4:11-12 (NLT)
11 Don't speak evil against each other, dear brothers and sisters.[a] If you criticize and judge each other, then you are criticizing and judging God's law. But your job is to obey the law, not to judge whether it applies to you. 12 God alone, who gave the law, is the Judge. He alone has the power to save or to destroy. So what right do you have to judge your neighbor?

Isaiah 54:17 (NLT)
17 But in that coming day no weapon turned against you will succeed.

Fill your paper with the breathings of your heart.
William Wordsworth

Living UNSTUCK

Aha Moments

Definition:

Aha Moment is a moment of sudden realization, inspiration, insight, recognition,
or comprehension.

Fill your paper with the breathings of your heart.   William Wordsworth

It is like whispering to one's self and listening at the same time.   Mina Murray

Forgiveness does not change the past, but it does enlarge the future. Paul Boese

Relying on God has to start all over everyday, as if nothing has yet been done. C.S. Lewis

But when I am afraid, I will put my trust in you. Psalm 56:3

Be still and know that I'm with you. Psalm 46:10

CPSIA information can be obtained
at www.ICGtesting.com
Printed in the USA
FSHW04n0344020318
45056FS

9 780999 179437